# THE VIETNAM VETERANS MEMORIAL
## Facts and Figures

Location: Constitution Gardens, Washington, D.C.

Length: 493.5 feet

Size and weight: 3,000 cubic feet, 175 pounds per cubic foot; Total weight of granite without foundation is 525,000 pounds

Date construction began: March 16, 1982

Date of dedication: November 13, 1982

Number of names on wall: 58, 156

Number of women's names: Eight

Cost: $7 million (approximately), all donated by the public

Number of contributors: More than 275,000 individuals

Type of stone: Black granite, mined near Bangalore, India; Finished in Vermont

Number of panels: 148, 2¾ inches thick, 40 inches wide; height varies from 8 inches to 10 feet, 1 inch

Date of plaza dedication: November 11, 1984 (Veterans Day)

## Cornerstones of Freedom

# The Story of

# THE VIETNAM VETERANS MEMORIAL

By David K. Wright

 CHILDRENS PRESS ®

CHICAGO

Millions of visitors have passed by the Vietnam Veterans Memorial.

Library of Congress Cataloging-in-Publication Data

Wright, David K.

The story of the Vietnam Veterans Memorial.
(Cornerstones of freedom)
Summary: The behind-the-scenes story of how and why the Vietnam
Veterans Memorial was built in Washington, D. C.
1. Vietnam Veterans Memorial (Washington, D.C.) —
Juvenile literature. 2. Washington (D.C.) — Buildings,
structures, etc. — Juvenile literature. I. Title.
II. Series.
DS559.83,W18W75  1989    959.704'38    89-713
ISBN 0-516-04745-0

There are hundreds of memorials in the city of Washington. They show presidents or heroic soldiers or famous patriots. Some, such as the Washington Monument and the Lincoln Memorial, tower impressively above the nation's capital.

But the memorial that attracts the most visitors is like no other statue or monument. It is a low, shiny, black wall covered with names.

This is the story of the Vietnam Veterans Memorial and how it was created.

The war in Vietnam ended for the United States in 1975 when the last American left that poor, bullet-scarred country. During the many years of fighting, more than 58,000 American soldiers died or were listed as missing. More than 300,000 were wounded or held prisoner.

America's involvement in the Vietnam war did not happen overnight. At first the government of South Vietnam asked America for only a few men to help train their army. Then the South Vietnamese began asking for more U.S. military leaders, more money, and more weapons. By the time the first big U.S. troopship landed in Vietnam in 1965, thousands of Americans were already helping South Vietnam in its war against North Vietnam.

Combat scenes like this were seen by millions on American television.

As American involvement in the war grew, so did the television, radio, newspaper, and magazine coverage. For the first time in history, Americans could know immediately all about fighting on the other side of the globe. Every day film, tape recordings, and stories were flown from the war zone to Japan, then sent to America by satellite.

Year in and year out, television viewers saw young Americans face death in steaming rice paddies, thick jungles, and ruined cities. Viewers had better ideas of the fighting than did most soldiers in Vietnam. The public was shown every horror of the war.

Many Americans protested U.S. involvement in the war.

This frightening information led many Americans to protest the war. There were antiwar demonstrations in American cities. At the time, American men over age 18 had to sign up for and serve in the armed forces. Some fled the country to avoid military duty. Others refused to sign up.

However, many Americans still supported the war. Not since the Civil War had the nation been so divided. Families were torn apart. Fathers turned against sons, husbands against wives, brothers against brothers.

As the war continued, more and more Americans opposed it. Finally, talks were held between South

In 1973 secret talks were held between the North Vietnamese and U.S. officials in Paris, France.

Vietnam and North Vietnam. The Americans began to pull their troops out of the war.

With all U.S. support gone, South Vietnam could not continue to hold out. North Vietnam took over South Vietnam on April 30, 1975.

The war was over. Americans who had believed in the war no longer wanted to talk about it. Americans who were against the war felt bad because they had been unable to stop years of killing. Many people on both sides wanted to forget the war.

But the war still haunted many of the 2.7 million

Jan C. Scruggs

Vietnam veterans. One vet who could not forget was Jan C. Scruggs. Scruggs had been sent to Vietnam from his Maryland home when he was only 19. He had seen heavy combat and had been wounded during his year in the tropical war. Scruggs had earned a medal for bravery. He wondered why no one thanked the living or paid tribute to the dead who had served in Vietnam.

Scruggs was neither for nor against the war. "I thought we were doing the right thing in Vietnam before I enlisted," he says. "But once I got there, I didn't keep that opinion. I lost enthusiasm for the war effort."

Much of his change of mind was due to South Vietnamese soldiers fighting alongside American troops. "They didn't appear to be real dedicated," Scruggs says. He began to wonder why he and his friends were fighting for people who didn't seem to care about their own country. This and other questions stayed with him and thousands of fellow Vietnam vets.

*The Deer Hunter* showed how the Vietnam war changed the lives of the men who fought in it.

One evening in 1979, Scruggs went to a movie. The movie was *The Deer Hunter*. It was one of the first motion pictures to deal with Vietnam. The film showed young Pennsylvanians, steel-mill workers, who left homes and jobs to fight the war. They were decent, everyday people—just like the Americans who served with Scruggs in Vietnam.

That night, he could not sleep. He was stunned by the fact that the service and sacrifice of ordinary men, living and dead, continued to be forgotten.

Scruggs made a decision that would affect millions: He would devote every extra minute to a memorial for Vietnam veterans. Others had similar thoughts, but Scruggs's plan was unique.

First, he decided that the memorial had to show the name of every American soldier who had died or remained missing in Vietnam. Second, it had to be something every American would accept. Third, the memorial would be built without spending a penny of government money. Fourth, it would be in Washington, D.C., to make the memorial truly national.

Scruggs was very enthusiastic, but he lacked experience. "I thought that raising the money would be easy," he said. A friendly reporter told him to hold a news conference. Scruggs did not know how much money he might need. But he told reporters that his only problem might be too much money from too many people!

Sadly, too much money wasn't the problem. After several weeks, donations totaled just $144. It appeared that a memorial to Vietnam veterans would never be built. Perhaps all the American people wanted to do was forget.

This lack of enthusiasm was noticed by several Vietnam veterans. Among them were two attorneys, Robert W. Doubek and John Wheeler. Doubek and Wheeler helped Scruggs start the Vietnam Veterans Memorial Foundation. Doubek became the executive director and the first employee of the non-profit organization.

The officers of the memorial fund met with Bob Hope to discuss fund-raising. From the left: Bob Hope, Bob Doubek, John Wheeler, Bob Frank, and Jan C. Scruggs.

Their aim was not to make money for themselves. Instead, the three wanted to find people who would donate money and to use the money to build a memorial.

The Vietnam Veterans Memorial Foundation set several goals. The first was to find a place for the memorial. Second, a design would be chosen. After the memorial was built, it would be dedicated. The men wanted dedication to take place on November 11, 1982, Veterans Day. That was just three years away.

The new organization had vowed to raise its own money. But no amount of money could purchase land

Senator Charles Mathias (left). Above, from left to right,
Jan Scruggs, Bill Jayne, Bob Doubek, and Sandy Mayo
met with Max Cleland, Administrator of Veterans Affairs.
Cleland was injured in Vietnam.

the government owned. That would have to be
donated. So the young veterans turned to U.S. Senator Charles Mathias—a Republican from Maryland
who had opposed American involvement in Vietnam.

Mathias believed that a tribute to Vietnam
veterans could help heal differences between
Americans. So he surprised and pleased the Vietnam Veterans Memorial Foundation organizers by
picking a two-acre site midway between two famous
capital landmarks: the Washington Monument and
the Lincoln Memorial.

Senator Mathias introduced a bill for the site to
become a memorial. All one hundred U.S. Senators
helped sponsor the legislation. It was passed on June
30, 1980. A similar bill was passed in the U.S. House
of Representatives.

Bob Doubek, Senator John Warner, and Jan Scruggs (left) accept a donation from the Hughes Aircraft representative. H. Ross Perot (right) gave $10,000.

Meanwhile, Senator John Warner of Virginia gave $1,000 of his own money and helped round up more. Senator Warner had supported the war. His support helped show that the memorial would be acceptable to all Americans. By the end of 1979, $9,000 had been raised. The biggest donation was $2,500 from the Veterans of Foreign Wars. The money was used to open a tiny office and to mail thousands of pleas for more donations.

Start-up money was given by companies doing business with the government and by private citizens. One of the major donors was a Texan, H. Ross Perot. The $10,000 he gave helped pay for postage, envelopes, appeal letters, and more. Vietnam Veterans Memorial Foundation members quickly learned that they needed money to raise money.

As donations began to come in, the money was put in the bank. The founders wondered how they would find an artist to create a great memorial. Neither Scruggs, Wheeler, nor Doubek had any specific ideas about how the memorial should look. But they saw the memorial as a place, rather than a monument. Scruggs insisted that the names of the dead be part of the design. No one disagreed.

The fund-raisers decided to hold a design contest. They invited people everywhere to enter their ideas of how the memorial should look.

Meanwhile, on July 1, 1980, President Jimmy Carter signed the bill that approved the site on the grassy Washington Mall for the memorial. Several government agencies were to approve the design. There was only one other rule in the legislation— that no dirt be moved until there was enough money to complete the job.

The vets had to decide on rules for the design. At first, they wanted to pick the design themselves. But they were neither artists nor experts in monument construction. They thought of putting together a group made up entirely of Vietnam veterans. But that would take time and those people would know little or nothing about memorial design or construction.

So the founders decided to find judges who were the most experienced and well-known people in the

Entries were displayed in an airplane hangar at Andrews Air Force Base, left. Paul D. Spreiregen (right), standing, the professional advisor for the design competition meets with the judges: Grady Clay, former editor *Landscape Architecture* magazine; Richard Hunt, sculptor; Harry M. Weese, architect; Hideo Sasaki, landscape architect; Pietro Belluschi, architect; Garrett Eckho, landscape architect; James Rosati, sculptor; and Constantino Nivola, sculptor.

country. The artists and designers they asked were eager to serve on the judging panel.

Sculptors and artists quickly learned of the competition. More than 5,000 copies of design rules were sent out. Over 1,400 entries came in by the deadline. The drawings and explanations eventually filled an airplane hangar at a nearby U.S. Air Force base. The veterans had raised nearly $2 million when the judges began to check the art entries.

All of the judges agreed that there were hundreds of great designs. "But one continues to haunt me,"

Bob Doubek poses with Maya Lin. Her design was selected over the more than 1,400 entries that had been submitted by the deadline.

an art expert told the veterans. This "haunting" entry was the work of a female college student. Her name was Maya Ying Lin.

Maya Lin grew up in a small Ohio town and is of Chinese descent. She had thought of her entry while taking a class in memorial design at college. The judges were impressed with its simplicity and strength. It was a low, black, shiny, chevron-shaped wall.

But it was more than that. The wall was to be a series of granite slabs, cut into the earth on the mall rather than rising out of it. Appearing almost like a rock formation, the wall would rise like a wedge to a height of more than 10 feet before angling back into the ground. It was to be 500 feet long.

The design was explained to members of the Vietnam Veterans Memorial Foundation. They were excited that the slabs would list the names of their 58,156 dead or missing comrades. The judges all recommended the design of 21-year-old Maya Lin.

Meanwhile, money was being raised in large amounts. A Virginia radio station held a pledge drive that brought in $250,000. The American Legion launched a fund-raising campaign among its hundreds of thousands of members. And people as far away as San Antonio, Texas, and Little Rock, Arkansas, collected money and sent it to VVMF headquarters.

The founders were busy, too. They hired an architect to manage construction and they made sure that the memorial could be used by the handicapped. Especially important, Robert Doubek ensured that the list of names was correct.

The names presented a problem. Hand carving them into the slabs of stone would take three years and cost $10 million. Doubek feared that the project might stall.

But in the summer of 1981 he received a call from

Larry Century adds a name to the wall.

a young Cleveland, Ohio, inventor named Larry Century. Century had come up with a way to stencil each name permanently on the granite. Scruggs, Doubek, and Wheeler began to believe that the project would continue problem-free. They were wrong.

That fall, the founders went to a meeting of the Fine Arts Commission. They were there for approval of the kind of stone they wanted for the memorial. Instead, they were met by an angry Vietnam veteran. He had entered an unsuccessful design in the memorial competition. Wearing medals earned in Vietnam, the veteran called Maya Lin's design a "black gash of shame and sorrow."

William Westmoreland

James Watt

The controversy grew. Many people liked the black wall. One was General William Westmoreland, who had commanded U.S. forces in Vietnam. Others included thousands of members of the Veterans of Foreign Wars and the American Legion. Also supportive were Gold Star Mothers. These women had lost sons in Vietnam and in other wars.

Opposing the design were some Vietnam veterans, newspaper columnists, and several organizations. Some people called the wall "a degrading ditch," or worse. These protesters wanted James Watt, secretary of the interior, to veto the project. Others wanted the wall color

Jan Scruggs and Gary Wright, project engineer, review the plans.

changed from black to white—even though memorials to the Marines and the Seabees are black.

Doubek, Scruggs, and Wheeler listened to these complaints, but felt they had no right to alter Maya Lin's design without her approval. The disagreement over design continued.

To complete the memorial by Veterans Day 1982, ground had to be broken in March 1982. The tension grew, but so did funds for the memorial. The American Legion's fund-raising campaign alone totaled one million dollars. Despite this growing support, James Watt said he would veto the project unless all sides agreed on the design.

Maya Lin in her New York office

A Senate hearing on the Vietnam Veterans Memorial became a showdown. Scruggs, Doubek, Wheeler, and their friends were outnumbered. The founders offered to put an American flag near the memorial, but that wasn't enough. Finally, after long arguments, a compromise was reached. Scruggs and his friends agreed to add a flag and a statue to the memorial site.

Throughout the months of controversy, Maya Lin was almost forgotten. She was too young to recall much about the war, and she was hurt that her design had been chosen and then criticized. If she had wanted flags or statues, she would have added them, she said.

Workers prepared the granite panels. The panels list the names of 58,156 individuals who were either killed or listed as missing in action in Vietnam. More than 275,000 individuals contributed money to the Vietnam Veterans Memorial.

Watt issued his approval on March 11, but he added a surprise sentence. He said the memorial could not be dedicated until the statue was finished.

Work began on the Washington Mall on March 15. A ground-breaking ceremony was held March 26. A committee was formed to choose a sculpture and decide where the statue and the Stars and Stripes should be placed.

The committee placed the flag and the statue at the entrance plaza some distance from the wall. The statue design they chose shows three soldiers, slightly larger than life, looking as if they had just been in a Vietnam war battle. They are dressed in jungle fatigues. They carry weapons and they look real, down to their dog tags.

Plans for the dedication continued. So did work on the wall. But it became clear that the statue could not be ready in time. Final approvals were made October 13, less than a month before Veterans Day.

Frederick Hart, the sculptor, had said from the start that he could not finish the statue by November. He began to work as the first granite panel was put in place in July.

Across America, people who read and heard about the memorial and people who donated were excited.

Thousands of veterans and their friends and families made plans to be in Washington for the dedication. Most national veterans' groups put pressure on James Watt to change his mind about the dedication. Once the sculpture was approved, the secretary relaxed his rule about dedicating everything at once. All systems were go—or were they?

About 150,000 people attended the dedication ceremonies on November 13, 1982.

There were still people who disliked the way the memorial looked. These people tried to overrule the Fine Arts Commission.

Quick work by Senator Mathias, who had found the site for the memorial, prevented the Commission's decision from being overruled. The statue and the flag stayed in the entrance plaza. The plans for the dedication continued.

"Dedication" is too mild a word for the weekend of November 13-14, 1982. Vietnam veterans, once ashamed or sad or angry, hopped on buses, planes, and trains headed for the nation's capital. They were joined by parents who had lost sons, wives who had lost husbands, sisters who had lost brothers, and friends who had lost friends.

They filled the hotels and motels in the Washington, D.C., area and overflowed into private homes, parks, parked cars, and recreational vehicles. Many were easy to identify—they wore a piece of olive-drab or camouflage clothing or leather-and-canvas jungle boots. Or, sadly, they moved along on canes, crutches, or in wheelchairs.

A total of 150,000 veterans rallied that fall weekend in Washington. Before the dedication, there were many other events. Every veteran who could walk—and many who could not—marched in a huge parade led by retired General William Westmoreland.

Ever since its dedication people have come to pay their respects. Some visitors leave flowers. Others just quietly read the names. Every visitor gets something special out of this "haunting" memorial.

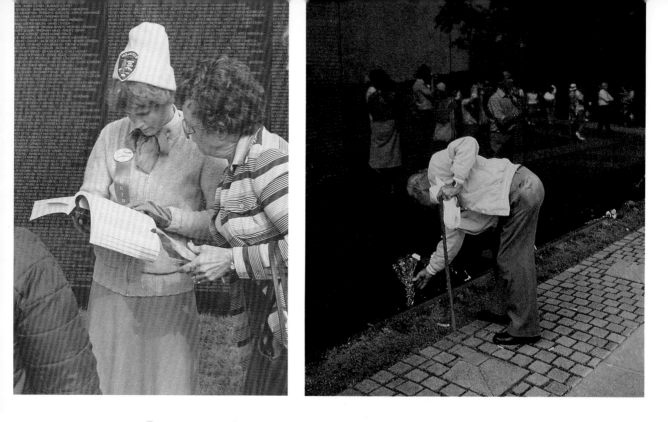

In a nearby church, visitors took turns reading the names of the dead. Friends and relatives waited for hours to hear a name they knew. Voices of the readers echoed with emotion. Elsewhere, men who had been in the cavalry, infantry, or artillery met in groups that were sometimes loud and happy, sometimes quiet and sad.

At the dedication, no one thought of the memorial as a "black gash of shame." Instead, veterans and other visitors were deeply moved. Visitors learned how to find a name, then walked to the correct panel and searched with their eyes. After finding the name, they touched it or stood silently and stared.

Tears were a part of the celebration. The tears

were for the people whose names were on the wall. But they were for living veterans, too. Tears were shed for vets hooked on drugs or in constant pain from old wounds or for those who had never rejoined society after leaving Vietnam.

The more visitors looked, the more they saw. The black granite wall reflected faces, grass, falling leaves, and blue sky. No one realized, during months of controversy, that anything so simple could be so dramatic. Those who opposed the wall were suddenly silent.

Maya Lin was impressed. The first time she saw it, she was startled at how much it was like her original idea. Lin had insisted all along that the names be on the wall in the order they had died. This made sense, since there were 15 Thomas Smiths, for example. Alphabetical order would have created a jumble of names.

The names of the dead are easy to find. They are listed alphabetically in five identical directories placed along nearby walkways. A listing looks like this:

John Philip Matlock   KY   47E   23

This soldier, the book shows, was from Kentucky. His name is on panel 47E. The "E" stands for east. It is on the 23rd line from the top. His name is one of 58,156 names on the wall.

Jan Scruggs had insisted from the start that the wall be nonpolitical. His convictions led to a prologue and an epilogue that are very simple.

Here is the prologue:

> In honor of the men and women of the Armed Forces of the United States who served in the Vietnam War. The names of those who gave their lives and of those who remain missing are inscribed in the order they were taken from us.

The epilogue is equally short and sincere:

> Our nation honors the courage, sacrifice, and devotion to duty and country of its Vietnam veterans. This memorial was built with private contributions from the American people.

By the end of 1988, the number of visitors to the site was more than 20 million. Unlike visitors at other monuments, people bring gifts to the wall.

This tradition began even before the wall was

completed: the brother of a lost pilot put a Purple Heart in the wall's foundation. Since then, people have left flags, letters, photos, patches and decals, medals and ribbons, and more. The National Park Service carefully saves these thousands of items. The memorial, said a Park Service employee, has become a "sacred site."

The memorial certainly has had a lasting effect on the men who helped create it. Doubek and Scruggs feel that it has changed their lives.

Scruggs still visits the memorial once or twice a month. He switched careers after the wall was completed. "After the memorial was finished, I didn't know what to do with myself," he says.

Doubek also visits the wall frequently. He helped start The Friends of the Vietnam Veterans Memorial. This organization aims to further the good that has come from the memorial.

Scruggs still gets a patriotic message from the wall—and from the sculpture and flag in the plaza. "It's important to serve your country when there's a crisis," he says. "But I feel those of us who served were somewhat betrayed by our country. The government was not honest with its own people."

Nevertheless, he thinks that "it's important to understand and be involved in our government. That will prevent unjust wars in the future and help elect people wise enough to avoid war altogether."

31

About the Author

David K. Wright is a freelance writer who lives in Wisconsin. He grew up in and around Richmond, Indiana, and graduated from Wittenberg University in Springfield, Ohio, in 1966.

Wright received his draft notice the day after he graduated from college. He was inducted in September 1966 and arrived in Vietnam at Bien Hoa in March 1967. He served in the U.S. Army 9th Infantry Division as an armor crewman. Wright was stationed at Camp Bearcat, east of Saigon, and at Dong Tam in the Mekong Delta. He returned from Vietnam in March 1968 and was honorably discharged in September of that year.

David Wright has written books on Vietnam and Malaysia in the *Enchantment of the World* series published by Childrens Press. He also has written *War in Vietnam*, a four-volume history, for Childrens Press.